IMAGES
of Aviation

GRAND FORKS
AIR FORCE BASE

IMAGES
of Aviation

GRAND FORKS
AIR FORCE BASE

Lt. Col. George A. Larson, USAF (Ret.)

ARCADIA
PUBLISHING

Published by Arcadia Publishing
Charleston, South Carolina

Printed in the United States of America

Library of Congress Control Number: 2019937217

For all general information, please contact Arcadia Publishing:
Telephone 843-853-2070
Fax 843-853-0044
E-mail sales@arcadiapublishing.com
For customer service and orders:
Toll-Free 1-888-313-2665

Visit us on the Internet at www.arcadiapublishing.com

*To the men and women both past and present who have served
at Grand Forks Air Force Base—thank you for your service.*

CONTENTS

Acknowledgments   6

Introduction   7

1.   Air Defense: 1956–1983   11

2.   4133rd Strategic Wing and 319th Air Refueling Wing: 1958–1993   33

3.   321st Strategic Missile Wing: 1963–1999   53

4.   Safeguard Anti-Ballistic Missile System: 1967–1976   71

5.   Weapons Storage Area: 1956–2013   91

6.   Global Hawk and Predator B: 2011–Present   99

7.   Grand Forks Air Force Base Air Park: 1983–Present   111

8.   Grand Forks Air Force Base: 1956–Present   119

Bibliography   127

ACKNOWLEDGMENTS

I want to begin with the Air Force Book Program in New York City, New York, which approved my request to travel to and research the history of Grand Forks Air Force Base (AFB), North Dakota. The secretary of the Air Force provided assistance to retrieve information from the Department of the Air Force Historian Office. I was assisted by the Air Force Air Combat Air Command and Air Force Global Strike Command to research information on the Minuteman intercontinental ballistic missiles (ICBM). The 319th Air Base Wing public affairs and historian provided access to their photographic archives to reconstruct the base's history as well as a tour of the installation. The Cold War history of the base was provided by the Air Force Historical Research Agency at Maxwell Air Force Base, Alabama. I was assisted in where to travel in eastern North Dakota to look for existing remains of former Cold War military sites by the Grand Forks Chamber of Commerce. The Ronald Reagan Minuteman Missile State Historic site's Oscar-Zero missile alert facility and the November-33 launch facility are the last remains of the 321st Missile Wing, a cluster of missile launch facilities and missile alert facilities spread over an area of approximately 6,500 square miles around Grand Forks AFB. Without their assistance, I would not have been able to reconstruct the history of the Minuteman ICBMs at Grand Forks. I especially want to thank many private landowners for allowing me access into the former Safeguard Anti–Ballistic Missile sites. Finally, small-town residents in eastern North Dakota took me to former Cold War sites near their towns that would have been nearly impossible to locate. Without all these agencies and contacts, the story of Grand Forks AFB would not have been possible.

INTRODUCTION

During the early 1950s, as the Cold War between the United States and the Soviet Union continued and appeared to be heading toward a nuclear confrontation, the US Air Force released information that it planned to build an Air Defense Command fighter-interceptor squadron base in eastern North Dakota. The Department of Defense selected Grand Forks AFB as a site for a new Air Defense Command installation in 1954, and citizens of the city of Grand Forks donated funds toward the purchase of 5,400 acres 15 miles west of the city. Grand Forks is located in the drainage area of the Red River Valley, near the forks of the Red Lake River and Red River to the north. Because of the junction of the two rivers, Grand Forks has suffered periodic flooding, sometimes surviving disaster by support from volunteers from Grand Forks AFB. Contractors began construction of the base on September 1, 1955, and it was named on December 1, 1955. Runway construction started on February 5, 1962, originally planned to be 12,350 feet. During that same month, the Air Force announced it planned to build up Grand Forks AFB to support Strategic Air Command (SAC) bombers and tankers as well as Air Defense Command fighter-interceptors. An interesting part of this air defense from the base at Grand Forks was the civilian Ground Observer Corps, prior to the building and operation of radar sites.

On February 8, 1957, the Air Defense Command activated the 486th Fighter Group on Grand Forks AFB. The fighter group served as host unit for a fighter-interceptor squadron, Air Defense Sector operations, and SAC units. In December 1957, the Air Force activated the Grand Forks Air Defense Sector of the North American Air Defense Command. This sector became operational with the Semi-Automatic Ground Environment (SAGE) system to cover air space of North Dakota, South Dakota, Minnesota, and the Canadian province of Manitoba. It was the most ambitious computer design and implementation project undertaken by the US military in the early 1950s. The project required the expertise of over 800 programmers and technicians to complete and implement, and resulted in the construction of 23 hardened bunkers at strategic locations around the United States (including North Dakota at Minot Air Force Base and Grand Forks AFB), with one additional bunker in Canada. The centers were designed to detect atomic weapon–carrying Russian long-range bombers and guide US fighter-interceptors, supported by surface to air missiles, to stop them. The computers used vacuum tubes, state-of-the-art computer design in 1963. Grand Forks AFB was also part of the manned fighter-interceptor commitment to the aerial defense of the northern United States from 1957 to 1974, under the responsibility of the 478th Fighter Group. It flew the supersonic F-101B Voodoo interceptor to provide fast interception of any unidentified aerial targets detected by area radar sites reporting to its four-story concrete SAGE blockhouse. In the 1960s, especially leading up to and after the Cuban Missile Crisis, the fear of a nuclear attack by the Soviet Union was considered likely.

In the meantime, SAC activated the 4133rd Strategic Wing (Provisional) as a tenant unit on Grand Forks AFB on September 1, 1959. SAC organized the 905th Air Refueling Squadron (Heavy) on February 1, 1960. The 905th Air Refueling Squadron received its first Boeing KC-135A

Stratotanker on May 6, 1960. On May 1, Air Defense Command transferred the 18th Fighter-Interceptor Squadron with its McDonnelll F-101 Voodoos from Wurtsmith Air Force Base, Michigan, to Grand Forks. On December 28, 1960, Air Defense Command activated the 478th Fighter Wing, Air Defense, replacing the 478th Fighter Group. Besides operating the base, the 478th Fighter Wing controlled F-101 operations of the 18th Fighter-Interceptor Squadron.

On January 1, 1962, SAC transferred the 30th Bombardment Squadron from Homestead Air Force Base, Florida, to Grand Forks AFB, assigning it to the 4133rd Strategic Wing. The 30th Bombardment Squadron received its first Boeing B-52H Stratofortress on April 29, 1962. On February 1, 1963, SAC organized the 319th Bombardment Wing on Grand Forks. The 319th Bombardment Wing replaced the inactivated 4133rd Strategic Wing. SAC assigned the 905th Air Refueling Squadron and 46th Bomb Squadron to the 319th Bombardment Wing. The 30th Bombardment Squadron was inactivated on the same day, with Air Defense Command handing over command and control of the base to SAC. The Air Force inactivated the Grand Forks Air Defense Sector and 478th Fighter Wing in 1963. Despite the change of operational command and control, the 18th Fighter-Interceptor Squadron continued to operate on Grand Forks. From July 1, 1963, to October 21, 1964, the 219th Bombardment Wing took over the responsibilities as host unit on the base.

Numerous organizational changes occurred on Grand Forks AFB during 1964. SAC activated the 840th Combat Support Group to assume duties as the host unit on August 19 and stationed the 4th Air Division on the base. On September 1, SAC activated the Strategic Aerospace Division on Grand Forks. In November, SAC organized the 321st Strategic Missile Wing while construction started on the Minuteman II ICBM complex. The 321st Strategic Missile Wing became operational to administrate, man, and operate the Minuteman II in December 1966.

Grand Forks AFB experienced several major changes in the 1970s. The first was the inactivation of the 18th Fighter-Interceptor Squadron on April 15, 1971. SAC transferred the 4th Strategic Air Division to Francis E. Warren Air Force Base, Wyoming, on June 30, 1971, and tasked the 321st Strategic Missile Wing to assume command over the 804th Combat Support Group and host unit responsibilities on July 1, 1971. Air Defense Command stationed the 460th Fighter-Interceptor Squadron on the base on July 30 with a squadron of Convair F-106 Delta Darts beginning alert operations. The 804th Combat Support Group was inactivated on July 31, 1972. During this time, construction started on 321st Strategic Missile Wing launch facilities and launch control centers to transition from the Minuteman II to Minuteman III ICBMs. This upgrade was completed on March 8, 1975. In 1974, the 460th Fighter-Interceptor Squadron won first place at the William Tell air-to-air competition at Eglin Air Force Base, Florida. Air Defense Command inactivated the squadron as part of a restructuring of its air defense system.

In 1983, the 319th Bombardment Wing swapped its Boeing B-52Hs for B-52Gs, with updated offensive avionics. On December 4, 1986, B-52Gs departed the base, replaced by B-1B Lancers in 1987. On June 16, 1988, SAC stationed the 42nd Air Division on the base. The division assumed host responsibilities, replacing the 321st Strategic Missile Wing in that role.

In 1991, SAC made significant organizational changes with the inactivation of the 42nd Air Division on July 9, assigning host responsibilities to the 319th Bomb Wing. On September 1, the 319th Bomb Wing was designated the 319th Wing, 321st Strategic Missile Wing. On June 1, 1992, the Air Force realigned its major commands, component command weapons systems, and missions. Tactical Air Command became Air Combat Command, Military Airlift Command became Air Mobility Command, with part of SAC's operations integrated into Air Force Space Command. The major command changes and weapon systems consolidations transformed Grand Forks AFB. With the combination or consolidation of combat air forces with Air Combat Command, the 319th Wing became an Air Combat Command unit. The 319th Wing became the 319th Bomb Wing. The wing's KC-135Rs, assigned to the 905th Air Refueling Squadron, were assigned to the 43rd Air Refueling Wing at Malmstrom Air Force Base, Montana. The 905th Air Refueling Squadron continued to operate from the base. The Air Force assigned the 321st Missile Wing from Air Combat Command to Air Force Strike Command on July 1, 1993. The wing was designated the 321st Missile Group on July 1, 1994.

On October 1, 1993, the 319th Bomb Wing became the 319th Air Refueling Wing, assigned to Air Mobility Command. During the transition to Air Mobility Command, the Air Force assigned the 906th, 911th, and 912th Air Refueling Squadrons to the 319th Air Refueling Wing. The 905th Air Refueling Squadron also came under the 319th. The 46th Bombardment Squadron joined the 319th Bomb Group. A more significant change occurred on May 26, 1994, when the last B-1B departed the base, followed by the inactivation of the 319th Bomb Group on July 16, 1994.

The Air Force made the formal announcement that it would remove 150 Minuteman III ICBMs with the inactivation of the 321st Missile Wing on July 2, 1998. The wing's Minuteman IIIs were shipped to other missile wings, with its silos going into caretaker status. On October 6, 1999, Grand Forks missile silos began to be imploded as required under the US and Soviet Strategic Arms Reduction Treaty. Site Oscar-Zero was sealed and transferred to the State of North Dakota as a historic installation named the Ronald Reagan Minuteman Missile State Historic Site.

One of the most notable events was the 1996–1997 winter weather, harsh and brutal even for North Dakota. Six blizzards dumped over 100 inches of snow on Grand Forks AFB and the surrounding area. The melting snow in the spring created the worst flooding in the state's history. Personnel from the 321st Missile Group and 318th Air Refueling Wing helped protect the city from rising floodwaters and opened the base to over 6,000 area residents.

On August 24, 2001, the base runway closed for repairs. This forced aircraft operations from June through November to the Fargo International Airport and to Fairchild Air Force Base, Washington. Although temporarily relocated, the four KC-135 squadrons continued to meet Air Force and Department of Defense missions.

On September 11, 2001, when terrorists attacked the United States, the 319th Air Refueling Wing stood as a Quick Reaction Alert Force in support of Operation Noble Eagle One. Later that month, the wing deployed to support Operation Enduring Freedom.

On July 13, 2004, a new $10 million Air Force commissary opened. In April 2005, Pres. George W. Bush authorized a round of base realignments and closures. These directed realignment of the 319th Air Refueling Wing's KC-135s to other Air Force tanker units but retained Grand Forks AFB as an active base. The 911th Air Refueling Squadron was affected by 2005 base realignment and closure recommendations with its inactivation on June 30, 2007, ending 13 years of service on Grand Forks.

The base continued to search for a viable mission, and in early 2009, US Customs and Border Protection (CBP) became a tenant organization on the base. The agency brought its unmanned aerial vehicle program to Grand Forks. Its unarmed, reconnaissance variant of the Predator unmanned aerial vehicle is one part of CBP's mission to secure America's borders, stopping illegal commerce and preventing terrorist attacks. The decision was made to operate from Grand Forks and not from Minot AFB due to a relatively clear flight line.

On October 1, 2009, the 906th Air Refueling Squadron transferred to the Air National Guard. Grand Forks AFB held a "mission complete" ceremony on June 19, 2009, to recognize the squadron's 15 years of outstanding air refueling operations. The 319th Air Refueling Wing said goodbye to the 912th Air Refueling Squadron on October 1, 2010, when the squadron transferred to March Air Reserve Base, California. On December 4, 2010, the final 905th Air Refueling Squadron's KC-135 departed Grand Forks for the 22nd Air Refueling Wing at McConnell AFB, Kansas, ending 50 years of air refueling presence on the base.

On December 31, 2010, the Air Force inactivated six operational units assigned to Grand Forks AFB: 319th Operations Group, 319th Maintenance Group, 905th Air Refueling Squadron, 319th Maintenance Operations Squadron, 319th Aircraft Maintenance Squadron, and 319th Maintenance Squadron. The 319th Operations Support Squadron was realigned with the 319th Air Refueling Wing. Personnel assigned to Detachment 1, 9th Reconnaissance Wing, arrived on base. Their arrival signaled the operational status of the Global Hawk unmanned surveillance aircraft mission under 2005 base realignment and closure recommendations for future operations on Grand Forks. Detachment 1 received its first commander on May 23, 2001, followed by the arrival of the first Global Hawk on June 2. Detachment 1 became the 9th Reconnaissance Group with two operational squadrons: one flying and one maintenance.

The Grand Sky Development Company operates a 50-year lease in the former Boeing B-52 Stratofortress bomber and Boeing KC-135 Stratotanker nuclear alert area, separated from the base. In cooperation with Grand Forks AFB, the unmanned aircraft vehicle technology park has access to the main runway for flight operations after clearance from the control tower. In March 2009, the University of North Dakota negotiated with the base commander, through Air Force and command channels, to allow the university to install and operate an unmanned aerial surveillance pilot, engineer, and support staff program. The university's Center for Excellence became operational in 2011.

Grand Sky Development Company is creating a technological hub in cooperation with commercial companies such as Northrop Grumman and the University of North Dakota for research, development, testing, production/maintenance, and pilot training of unmanned aerial vehicles for civilian applications.

One

AIR DEFENSE
1956–1983

By 1956, the US military considered North Dakota vital to the nation's defense and aircraft warning system. On the 12,350-foot runway at Minot AFB, Air Defense Command could operate fighter-interceptors, and SAC could operate bombers and tankers. On February 8, 1957, Air Defense Command activated the 478th Fighter Group. This unit would serve as the host unit for a fighter-interceptor squadron and an Air Defense Sector operation, and as home to SAC units. In December 1957, the Air Force activated the Grand Forks Air Defense Sector, North American Air Defense. This sector became operational with the SAGE system on December 15, 1959. The 18th Fighter-Interceptor Squadron was transferred from Wurtsmith AFB to Grand Forks on May 1, 1969, equipped with the McDonnelll F-101B Voodoo supersonic fighter-interceptor. To direct these fighters, the SAGE system was built, a continental air defense network funded by the US military. The SAGE system, at the time, was the most ambitious computer design and implementation project ever undertaken by the US military. Fighter-interceptors stationed at Grand Forks were controlled by SAGE and ground control intercept radar operators. After 1983, when the SAGE system was shut down, the 91st Strategic Missile Wing used the former SAGE building as its headquarters until it was torn down in 2003, replaced by a modern, more functional building.

Finley Air Force Station was part of the SAGE system for Grand Forks AFB. Construction on the radar station began in late 1948, and it became operational in 1950 and was designated an aircraft control and warning squadron. It operated as the 785th Radar Squadron, part of the SAGE system when that system became operational. The radar station was equipped with state-of-the-art electronic equipment.

Part of the early air defense system managed at Grand Forks was the Ground Observer Corps, scanning the skies for Russian bombers. The fear of a Russian attack led to the development of a civil defense program.

There were never enough civilian volunteers to man the Ground Observer Corps post for two-hour shifts for 24-hour coverage. The general attitude in North Dakota was that there was no danger of attack from Russia and most people could not see the need for observation posts to scan the horizon for possible Russian bombers. The Air Force erected advertising billboards like this one to attract volunteers. (Courtesy of the North Dakota State Historical Society.)

During World War II, this poster and others were used to recruit volunteers for the Ground Observer Corps, scanning for enemy aircraft along the borders. These threats did not exist, but fear of another attack after Pearl Harbor was everywhere. In the 1950s, the threat from Russian nuclear attack seemed imminent, and volunteers were urgently needed. (Author's collection.)

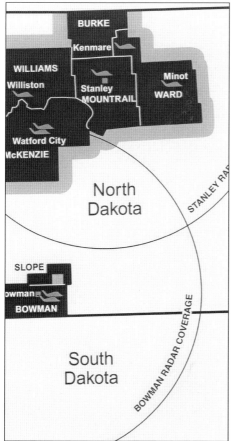

This map shows North Dakota's area of responsibility for the Ground Observer Corps. This area was deemed a likely corridor for Russian bombers coming in over the North Pole, through Canada, and into the northern United States. (Courtesy of the North Dakota State Historical Society.)

13

The Cold War–era Air Defense Command created this poster showing a husband and wife looking at an unidentified aircraft flying overhead. He has binoculars, and she is wearing a headset to communicate with their filter center personnel, shown in the inset. (Author's collection.)

In open areas throughout northern North Dakota, wherever possible, small elevated wooden structures were built to protect Ground Observer Corps scanners from the weather, which was hot in the summer and cold in the winter. (Courtesy of the North Dakota State Historical Society.)

A prototype glass-enclosed Ground Observer Corps post is seen here under review by Air Force officers and North Dakota civil defense officials. The post was evaluated, but the expense for its production, transportation, and assembly was not in the air defense budget. (Courtesy of the North Dakota State Historical Society.)

When volunteer numbers did not meet demands for manning Ground Observer Corps posts, the Air Force switched to a patriotic appeal to attract North Dakota citizens to take two-hour shifts to scan for Russian bombers entering the state. (Courtesy of the North Dakota State Historical Society.)

Ground
Observers'
Guide

DEPARTMENT OF THE AIR FORCE

Each Ground Observer Corps post in North Dakota received this observers' guide with US and Russian aircraft silhouettes to help identify the type of aircraft spotted. (Author's collection.)

Clockwise from top left, information is plotted on a table map, following procedures developed by the British air force during World War II; a filter center receives information from its surrounding ground observer posts; and the closest Air Defense Command alert base is contacted to launch fighter-interceptors to visually identify the target. (Courtesy of the North Dakota State Historical Society.)

In May 1992, Russian air force aircraft visited Barksdale Air Base, Louisiana. The two turboprop aircraft behind the Boeing B-52H Stratofortress are Tu-95 Bear bombers, the type Ground Observer Corps were trained to identify. The large transport in the background is an AN-124 Condor, support aircraft for the Tu-95s. (Courtesy of the Barksdale Air Force Base Public Affairs.)

The open areas of North Dakota provided few cities for building large-capacity civil defense shelters. The state provided instructions on how to build earth covered bomb shelters, with supplies stored inside to allow a family to survive up to 14 days, the minimum estimated time before radiation levels dropped enough to allow short periods outside the shelters. Root cellars were converted into bomb shelters where available. (Courtesy of the North Dakota State Historical Society.)

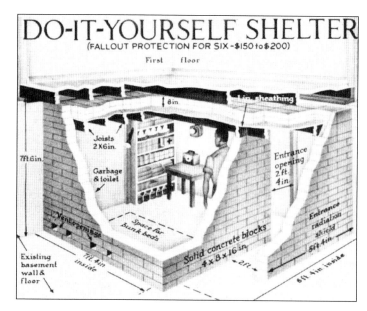

DO-IT-YOURSELF SHELTER
(FALLOUT PROTECTION FOR SIX ~ $150 to $200)

First floor

8in

4 in. sheathing

Joists 2 X 6 in.

7 ft 6 in.

Garbage & toilet

Entrance opening 2 ft. 4 in.

Vent openings

Space for bunk beds

Existing basement wall & floor

7 ft 4 in. inside

Solid concrete blocks 4 x 8 x 16 in.

2 ft

Entrance radiation shield

5 ft 4 in.

8 ft 4 in. inside

In larger cities such as Minot, Bismarck, Grand Forks, and Fargo, civil defense provided plans to residents to build a basement bomb shelter. Building supply companies packaged the construction materials, selling it as a complete package. It was suggested to position the bomb shelter in the northwest corner of the basement to provide protection from the expected direction of a Russian nuclear attack. (Courtesy of the North Dakota State Historical Society.)

Local newspapers and magazines used a hastily prepared information page, with fabric-covered boxes and wall hangings to show how cities could equipment a public fallout shelter with the minimum amount of survival supplies. These city fallout shelters were to be located in the basements of public buildings, hotels, and businesses. However, these buildings were not constructed to survive a nuclear blast. (Courtesy of the North Dakota State Historical Society.)

Private construction companies in North Dakota advertised bomb shelters, in which a family could live during and after a nuclear exchange with the Soviet Union and the expected civil unrest afterward. This flyer from a Minot construction company was typical. These structures were Federal Home Administration loan–approved. (Courtesy of the Minot Public Library.)

INSTALL THIS ALL-METAL 8x12 FOOT CAPSULE FOR YOUR FAMILY

It is strong enough to protect you and your family, it is small enough to be practical, it is large enough for indefinite survival. This shelter is built of All Welded Steel Construction. It is one unit, which is buried underground, near your home, in the city or country.

ACT NOW!!! This Survival Capsule is equipped with water-tight escape latch, locked from inside, bunk bed brackets, toilet facilities, radio antenna, food storage compartments. You will be safe from the effects of fallout, radiation, safe from cave-ins of structures above. Eligible for FHA financing . . . Title 1 and Title 2 Loans. Investigate the Survival Capsule NOW. P.O. Box 1467, Great Falls, Mont. Phone GL 4-2361. 7 days a week, all day and evenings.

97% Can Survive a Nuclear War . . .
Provided we are Prepared Beforehand with . . .

URVIVAL SHELTERS

he SURVIVAL CAPSULE is the best on the market

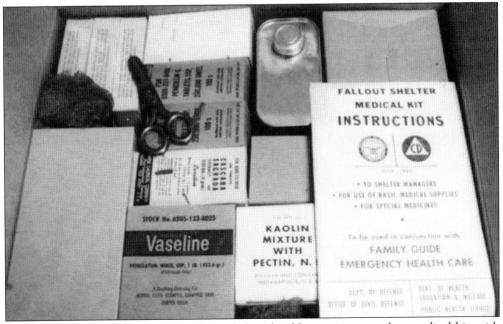

It was recommended that a family fallout shelter should contain a complete medical kit, with instructions on how to diagnosis and treat radiation-related conditions. After a nuclear attack, the chances of locating a doctor would be doubtful. (Author's collection.)

US civil defense provided a plan for elaborate family fallout shelters. Photographs of these types of shelters were distributed showing a large family inside, with bunk beds, canned food and water, games, waste disposal barrels, reading materials, extra clothes, and bedding. This father is hand-cranking an air-recycling purification system. Without this, the air inside could reach a high level of carbon dioxide and increased temperature. Lights were battery-powered. (Author's collection.)

In the early 1950s, after the Korean War, many North Dakota residents could not see any threat to them from the Soviet Union, but the Cuban Missile Crisis in 1962 changed this, and civil defense could not be ignored. Schoolchildren were taught "duck and cover" to protect them from a nuclear detonation. (Courtesy of the North Dakota State Historical Society.)

In large cities such as Grand Forks, civil defense authorities surveyed underground structures as sites of public fallout shelters. They were stocked with food, water, cots, medical supplies, lights, and whatever could be purchased with available funds. They were quickly abandoned, with many of the supplies stolen or vandalized. (Courtesy of the North Dakota State Historical Society.)

Construction on Grand Forks AFB included a concrete, two-bay fighter-interceptor alert facility on the south end of the runway. It had roll-in and roll-out capability, made possible by large garage-type doors at each end, which could be closed during cold weather. This allowed aircraft to be kept ready for a high-speed takeoff. (Courtesy of Grand Forks Air Force Base, 319th Air Base Wing Public Affairs.)

In 2013, the former Air Defense Command fighter-interceptor alert bay five remained, used as storage and general maintenance. (Author's collection.)

This 2014 aerial photograph, looking north at the base runway, shows the adjacent support area and hangars to the right. The runway is now for emergency landing only, used by unmanned aircraft on the base. (Courtesy of Grand Forks Air Force Base, 319th Air Base Wing Public Affairs.)

Seen here are two 460th Fighter-Interceptor Squadron Convair F-106A Delta Darts on the aircraft ramp, with wheels blocked and ground wire attached to prevent the buildup of static electricity, which could be dangerous to personnel around the aircraft. (Courtesy of Grand Forks Air Force Base, 319th Air Base Wing Public Affairs.)

A 460th Fighter-Interceptor Squadron F-106A is in the process of taking off on a training mission. This photograph highlights the clean appearance of the supersonic delta wing Air Defense Command fighter. (Courtesy of Grand Forks Air Force Base, 319th Air Base Wing Public Affairs.)

Two 460th Fighter-Interceptor Squadron F-106A are pictured during a routine training mission and public affairs photo opportunity. This photograph was taken from a squadron twin-seat F-106B flight trainer. (Courtesy of Grand Forks Air Force Base, 319th Air Base Wing Public Affairs.)

A Convair F-102A Delta Dagger assigned to the 460th Fighter Squadron is pictured parked on the flight line. The cockpit canopy is open. Aircraft often were parked wingtip to wingtip, and safety was always paramount to prevent damaging adjacent aircraft. (Courtesy of Grand Forks Air Force Base, 319th Air Base Wing Public Affairs.)

A Convair F-106A Delta Dart is on display at the National Museum of the US Air Force, Cold War Gallery. The internal bomb bay is open, with the cover lowered, showing three infrared-guided air-to-air missiles. The cockpit is closed. (Author's collection.)

Pictured is a 460th Fighter-Interceptor Squadron aircraft on the flight line. In the background, a Northrop F-89D Scorpion is on the runway. (Courtesy of Grand Forks Air Force Base, 319th Air Base Wing Public Affairs.)

Pictured is an 18th Fighter-Interceptor Squadron McDonnell F-101B Voodoo. The "B" variant was a two-seat interceptor. The aircraft is on a Grand Forks ramp. There is a crew ladder alongside the aircraft. The cockpit is open in preparation for a training mission. (Courtesy of Grand Forks Air Force Base, 319th Air Base Wing Public Affairs.)

Three 18th Fighter-Interceptor Squadron armaments personnel load two inert training Genie rockets onto the internal weapons platform of an F-101B Voodoo. The absence of armed security personnel, two officers who signed out a nuclear-tipped Genie rocket from the weapons storage area, and warning flags on the weapons indicate that these are inert rockets. (Courtesy of Grand Forks Air Force Base, 319th Air Base Wing Public Affairs.)

Pictured are two 18th Fighter-Interceptor Squadron F-101Bs airborne on a local training flight. This photograph was taken from another squadron aircraft flying slightly below and parallel. (Courtesy of Grand Forks Air Force Base, 319th Air Base Wing Public Affairs.)

This profile image of an 18th Fighter-Interceptor Squadron F-101B on the Grand Forks flight line shows the clear aerodynamic profile needed for a supersonic aircraft. (Courtesy of Grand Forks Air Force Base, 319th Air Base Wing Public Affairs.)

A former 18th Fighter-Interceptor Squadron F-101B is on static display in the Grand Forks airport, adjacent to the main entrance. (Author's collection.)

This F-101B is on display at the National Museum of the US Air Force, Cold War Gallery, fitted with two range-extending, droppable auxiliary fuel tanks. Two inert Genie rockets are visible below the aircraft on the internal weapons bay platform. (Author's collection.)

These decommissioned F-101Bs are in open temporary desert storage at Davis Monthan Air Force Base, 309th Aerospace Maintenance and Regeneration Group, Arizona, pending scrapping as excess federal assets. (Author's collection.)

Pictured is the SAGE building, Air Defense Command, in 1995 on Grand Forks AFB. After the SAGE network was deactivated, the computers and operating equipment were removed, with the building used as a command center and later abandoned after SAC's nuclear deterrence mission ended. (Courtesy of Geo-Marine Inc.)

The heart of the former SAGE building was two large vacuum tube central processing units, each with 60,000 tubes. One computer operated at a time, with the second as a backup. The two-floor building was the center of the Grand Forks AFB air defense operations. (Courtesy of Grand Forks Air Force Base, 319th Air Base Wing Public Affairs.)

This was the operations room inside the SAGE building, with two rows of cathode ray tube consoles, monitoring received radar plots from surrounding early warning radars. The consoles were operated by military and civilian personnel 24 hours a day. (Courtesy of Grand Forks Air Force Base, 319th Air Base Wing Public Affairs.)

The command section was manned 24 hours a day by officers to review and respond to possible airborne threats. These were projected onto a large screen, activated by a light gun (visible at right center), to determine what action would be taken, including the launching of fighter-interceptor aircraft. (Courtesy of Grand Forks Air Force Base, 319th Air Base Wing Public Affairs.)

An example of a SAGE radar system was Finley Air Force Station, one of the last batch of 23 such stations constructed as part of Air Defense Command's aircraft warning network, operational in late 1952. The large building supported the AN-FPS-35 radar on its roof. (Author's collection.)

Two

4133RD STRATEGIC WING AND 319TH AIR REFUELING WING
1958–1993

SAC activated the 4133rd Strategic Wing as a tenant unit at Grand Forks AFB on September 1, 1958, to prepare the base to operate Boeing B-52 Stratofortresses and KC-135A Stratotankers. On January 1, 1962, SAC transferred the 30th Bomb Squadron from Homestead AFB, Florida, to Grand Forks, assigning it to the 4133rd Strategic Wing. The 30th Bomb Squadron received its first B-52H on April 29, 1962. The Air Force activated the 319th Bomb Wing at Grand Forks on November 15, 1962. On February 1, 1963, SAC organized the 319th Bomb Wing, assigning it to the 4133rd Strategic Wing. The 319th Bomb Wing assumed the mission of training for emergency war operations and stepped up quick reaction alert forces with B-52Hs and KC-135As. The B-1A was first deployed in the late 1970s as a replacement for the B-52H, which is still operational. Grand Forks was equipped with B-1Bs in 1987. In December 1989, the 319th Bomb Wing flew combat air refueling missions in support of US forces during Operation Just Cause, the invasion of Panama. Later, the 319th Bomb Wing's tankers provided aerial refueling support during deployment of US forces to the Middle East during the US and coalition forces buildup to Operation Desert Shield in 1990, followed by supporting allied aircraft operations during Operation Desert Storm in 1991. In that year, Pres. George H. Bush decided to reduce the size of the US nuclear alert force. On September 28, the 319th Bomb Wing removed its B-1Bs and KC-135Rs from nuclear alert after nearly 30 years on Grand Forks AFB. With the inactivation of SAC on June 1, 1992, the 319th Bomb Wing was reassigned to Air Combat Command, 905th Air Refueling Wing was reassigned to the 305th Air Refueling Wing at Grissom Air Force Base, Indiana, and on July 1, 1993, to the 43rd Air Refueling Wing at Malmstrom AFB, Montana. In February 1993, Air Combat Command ended the wing's nuclear mission.

Pictured is the headquarters building for 319th Air Base Wing on Grand Forks AFB, north of the main drive into the base from the front gate. (Author's collection.)

Shown is the former Cold War bomber and aerial tanker alert area off the southwest end of the Grand Forks north-south runway. The security gate was deactivated in 2013 and is now closed due to the unmanned aircraft programs by Great Sky Development Company. (Author's collection.)

Around the former nuclear alert area, a high concrete wall was built to block direct view from roads to the south and west. The "A8" on the wall marked the location of one of the pad's nuclear alert parking aprons (now removed and under private ownership). (Author's collection.)

This is the large former aircraft alert parking area in 2013, with concrete intact, but the alert facility and security lights were demolished or removed after the base ceased nuclear alert operations. (Author's collection.)

After aircraft were removed from the base, a barrier wire fence was erected across the former high-speed alert taxiway to the south end of the runway, visible in the background. (Author's collection.)

After SAC became the primary tenant on Grand Forks AFB, large B-52–capable hangars were built for maintenance, with a cutout above the doors to allow the entire aircraft to be towed inside, except for the tail section. (Author's collection.)

Pictured is a large three-bay hangar, built to accommodate B-1B maintenance even in cold weather. The B-1B's tail fit in the notch above the door. (Author's collection.)

KC-135 Stratotanker hangars had a different appearance, with a padded half circle on the hangar doors, which closed around the tanker's rear fuselage ahead of the tail, closing off outside weather for maintenance work on the aircraft. (Author's collection.)

Grand Forks still has a secured flight line due to unmanned aerial vehicle operations, which requires controlled access by entering a passcode. There are no security patrols as there were during nuclear alert operations. (Author's collection.)

During the Cold War, one of the air-to-ground weapons carried by nuclear alert B-52s was the Hound Dog turbojet missile, one under each wing of the bomber, armed with a one-megaton warhead, allowing enemy defenses to be struck ahead and to either side of the bomber's flight path. This one is on display at the Grand Forks AFB Air Park. (Author's collection.)

This Boeing B-52G Stratofortress is on display in the base air park. The bomber was used during Operation Desert Storm against front line Iraqi troops to prepare for the allied ground offensive. (Author's collection.)

When B-52s and KC-135s were assigned to Grand Forks, a tall aircraft control tower was built to provide a 360-degree, unobstructed view of the runway, taxiway, and parking area. (Author's collection.)

Pictured is one of the former Cold War squadron bomber and tanker operations buildings on Grand Forks, with access onto the flight line for both pedestrians and vehicles to aircraft parked on the ramp. (Author's collection.)

The large aircraft parking ramp on Grand Forks had a row of blast deflectors, one at each parking spot, to redirect engine exhaust upward, reducing danger to aircraft and ground crew personnel nearby. (Author's collection.)

The 319th Bomb Wing initially flew the B-52H from 1963 to 1983, then re-equipped with the B-52G. Pictured is a B-52H on Ellsworth Air Force Base, South Dakota, during the Dakota Thunder 2009 open house. (Author's collection.)

This head-on view of a B-52H shows the aircraft's eight turbofan engines and slightly drooping wings, which lift during takeoff as airflow forces them up. The aircraft's large wing flaps are visible, along with an auxiliary fuel tank on each wing and outrigger wing support gear. (Author's collection.)

Shown are the four left TF33-P-3 turbofan engines on the B-52H, each rated at 17,000 pounds of thrust. The engine was cleaner, quieter, and more fuel efficient for longer range over the B-52G. (Author's collection.)

This is a close-up view of the B-52H's four landing gears, a quadricycle arrangement consisting of two-wheeled main units to accommodate the aircraft's weight, with a unique feature that allows the fuselage to turn into the wind while the landing gear points down the runway for landings during crosswinds. (Author's collection.)

Pictured is the B-52H's nose with the An/ASQ-151 Electromagnetic Optical View System, with a low-light TBVTO electro-optical viewing system unit and forward-looking infrared sensor. (Author's collection.)

This photograph of a B-52H with its wing flaps extended shows the shortened tail structure used on the B-52G and B-52H variants. (Author's collection.)

Here are the turbofan engine double clusters, auxiliary fuel tank, drooping wings, and outrigger wing support. (Author's collection.)

Pictured is the left side, under-wing heavy stores adapter beam, capable of carrying a variety of conventional bombs and precision-guided conventional and nuclear munitions. (Author's collection.)

The B-52H has an unlimited range with aerial refueling, as shown here from the rear window on a KC-135R Stratotanker. (Courtesy of the US Air Force.)

On January 27, 1983, a 319th Bomb Wing B-52G was undergoing post-flight maintenance of a fuel transfer valve fault, which was improperly performed, with the valve's motor igniting vapor inside the fuel tank. The resulting explosion destroyed the bomber before the fire could be extinguished. (Courtesy of Grand Forks Air Force Base, 319th Air Base Wing Public Affairs.)

Pictured is a 319th Bomb Wing B-52G airborne in the camouflage paint scheme used during bombing missions over Iraq. The bomb bay is open. (Courtesy of Grand Forks Air Force Base, 319th Air Base Wing Public Affairs.)

During aircraft transition on Grand Forks, for a short time, both the B-52G and B-1B operated from the base. (Courtesy of Grand Forks Air Force Base, 319th Air Base Wing Public Affairs.)

Pictured is a B-52G on the Grand Forks flight line. The bomb bay is open, with empty munitions loader behind, part of a munitions loading exercise. (Courtesy of Grand Forks Air Force Base, 319th Air Base Wing Public Affairs.)

This B-52H on the parking ramp displays the wide range of munitions the aircraft could carry, from conventional to nuclear. (Courtesy of the US Air Force.)

Shown is a B-1B on the base aircraft ramp. This was a public affairs photograph release, with a rainbow after a thunderstorm went through the base seen in the background. (Courtesy of Grand Forks Air Force Base, 319th Air Base Wing Public Affairs.)

Here is a close-up view of a B-1B on Ellsworth AFB, 28th Bomb Wing, in South Dakota, which operates the aircraft as one of two remaining B-1B bases. (Author's collection.)

This is another B-1B on Ellsworth AFB. The B-1B was developed in the 1970s to replace the B-52s, and now the B-52H is projected to remain flying until possibly 2050, with the B-1B replaced by the new long-range strike bomber, B-21, currently under development. (Author's collection.)

This view of a B-1B rear fuselage section shows the four 15,000-pound-thrust General Electric F1-GE-101 turbofan engine exhausts, with engine covers on, fully extended wings, and moveable tail surface. (Author's collection.)

Pictured is a B-1B taking off from Ellsworth's runway into a south wind. (Author's collection.)

The first Boeing KC-135A Stratotanker to land on Grand Forks was the "City of Grand Forks," also referred to as the "Spirit of North Dakota," assigned to the 319th Air Refueling Squadron. It is on display at the Grand Forks AFB Air Park. (Author's collection.)

Here is another view of KC-135A "City of Grand Forks," on display at the air park. (Author's collection.)

This row of 319th Air Refueling wing KC-135R Stratotankers on the Grand Forks AFB flight line were powered by the improved CFM-56 turbofan engines. (Courtesy of the Grand Force Air Force Base, 319th Air Base Wing Public Affairs.)

During a training exercise, four KC-135Rs are on the taxiway, moving to the end of the runway for a minimum interval takeoff procedure. (Courtesy of the Grand Forks Air Force Base, 319th Air Base Wing Public Affairs.)

During cold and snowy winter weather on Grand Forks, KC-135Rs required de-icing prior to takeoff in order to maintain proper flight characteristics. (Courtesy of Grand Forks Air Force Base, 319th Air Base Wing Public Affairs.)

Three

321ST STRATEGIC MISSILE WING
1963–1999

On July 1, 1963, Aerospace Defense Command transferred operational control of Grand Forks AFB to SAC in anticipation of the arrival on the 321st Strategic Missile Wing. On February 28, 1963, the Air Force announced that Morrison-Knudsen & Associates, which submitted a contract bid amount over $128 million, would serve as the primary contractor for the missile field. On November 1, 1964, the 321st Strategic Missile Wing was activated. In March 1965, the 321st Wing Headquarters moved into building 306, a 75-foot-high concrete blockhouse bunker and former Air Defense Command SAGE direction center. In August 1965, Grand Forks received its first Minuteman, transported to the base on a special railroad car from Assembly Plant 77 at Hill Air Force Base, Utah. In March 1966, the base received the first Minuteman II shipped in an Air Force C-141A, an Air Force first. The nuclear blast–hardened complex, 60 feet below the launch control support building, consisted of two separate pressurized structures. The launch control equipment building provides environmental control and power to the launch control center. In previous missile alert facility construction, this was aboveground, vulnerable to a nuclear attack. Inside is an emergency diesel-electric generator to provide continuous uninterrupted power if commercial power was cut off due to natural disaster or nuclear attack. As the first base to deploy the Minuteman II ICBM system, Grand Forks hosted Project Long Life II, a reliability test in which modified Minuteman missiles were provided a short solid-fuel capsule to allow it to clear the silo and travel a few hundred feet before the fuel was exhausted and the missile fell to the ground. From December 1971 to March 1973, the 321st Strategic Missile Wing transitioned to the Minuteman III. The Strategic Arms Reduction Treaty reduced strategic weapons for the United States and Russia, which closed missile operations for the 321st Strategic Missile Wing and led to the removal of its Minuteman IIIs and destruction of launch facilities and launch control centers.

Construction of a Minuteman launch facility was a massive undertaking. Construction started by excavating a 35-foot-deep trench with clam shovels and bulldozers, the soil stacked nearby for later backfill. Next, a large auger completed the excavation to a depth of 80 feet. (Courtesy of the US Air Force.)

A construction crew poured a concrete deflector pad at the shaft's bottom. A prefabricated steel liner, 25 tons and 26 feet long, was inserted into the shaft. Concrete was poured around the steel liner to a thickness of 12 inches. (Courtesy of the US Air Force.)

Shown is a launch facility, basically complete. For the missile field, contractors moved 20 million cubic yards of dirt for the 150 launch facilities and 15 missile alert facilities, and used 35,000 tons of steel and 150,000 cubic yards of concrete. (Courtesy of the US Air Force.)

Pictured is an aerial view of the completed Minuteman launch facility, secured by a chain-link fence and monitored by remotely operated security cameras from the missile alert facility, along with intrusion sensors and lights. The missile silo is the concrete structure at center, with adjacent underground support building. (Courtesy of the US Air Force.)

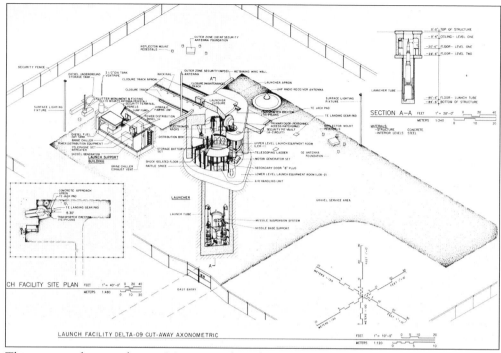

This cutaway drawing shows a Minuteman launch facility at Ellsworth AFB, Delta Flight. The launch facilities on Grand Forks AFB were constructed to similar plans. (Courtesy of the National Park Service.)

North Dakota officials turned a former 321st Missile Wing missile alert facility (Oscar-Zero) and launch facility (November-33) into the Ronald Reagan Minuteman Missile State Historic Site, saving an important Cold War nuclear deterrence site that protected the United States. (Author's collection.)

Shown is a low, buttressed concrete wing wall on each side of the launcher closure that separates the maneuver area from the ground below. A steel track on a concrete pad is positioned directly behind the launcher closure to support the heavy structure when opened. (Author's collection.)

The underground launch tube and equipment room are covered by a massive, reinforced concrete slab. The launcher closure is level with the surface to aid in nuclear detonation survival from overpressure and blast effects, three and a half feet thick, and weighing 90 tons. (Author's collection.)

This Minuteman III ICBM is on static display south of the entrance to Francis E. Warren AFB in Wyoming. (Author's collection.)

A specialized vehicle, the Boeing transporter/erector loader semitrailer and tractor, was used to transport Minuteman missiles to and from launch facilities and load and remove missiles as required. (Author's collection.)

Excavation of the launch control center and adjacent launch control equipment building was dug to a depth of 32 feet. These capsule walls were four-foot-thick concrete with a quarter-inch-thick steel plate. The launch control center was 59 feet long and 29 feet in diameter. (Courtesy of the US Air Force.)

This is a drawing of a launch control center and launch control equipment building, with the missile alert facility. (Courtesy of the US Air Force.)

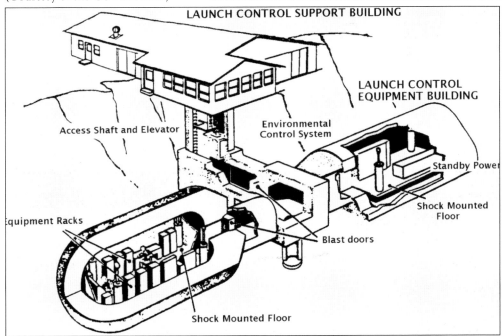

LAUNCH CONTROL SUPPORT BUILDING

LAUNCH CONTROL EQUIPMENT BUILDING

Access Shaft and Elevator

Environmental Control System

Standby Power

Shock Mounted Floor

Equipment Racks

Blast doors

Shock Mounted Floor

Pictured is the entrance to the Oscar-Zero missile alert facility at the Ronald Reagan Minuteman Missile State Historic Site in Cooperstown, North Dakota. It contains an unpretentious, one-story, ranch-style wood structure, with a low-pitched, side-gable roof and is considered non-survival in a nuclear exchange with the Soviet Union. (Author's collection.)

The Oscar-Zero launch control support building offered access to the underground launch control center and launch control equipment building. (Author's collection.)

The helicopter landing pad outside the security area of Oscar-Zero was used to deliver VIPs and the security forces tactical response team in response to intrusion alarms, as well as deliver mission-critical parts and equipment to the missile alert facility. (Author's collection.)

This 1980s style kitchen inside the launch control support building provided hot meals for the site's personnel and visitors. (Author's collection.)

This recreation room inside the launch control support building contained a pool table and table tennis tables, foosball table, comfortable chairs for reading and relaxing, and computer. (Author's collection.)

The launch control support building bedrooms were equipped with bunk beds for onsite, above-ground personnel, visiting maintenance crews, and VIP visitors. (Author's collection.)

This was the launch control support building facilities manager's separate bedroom. (Author's collection.)

Access down into the underground launch control center and launch control equipment building and aboveground onsite security is controlled from the security control center. It is equipped with communications and monitoring equipment. (Author's collection.)

Security force personnel in the security control center could look out the windows, observing the facility entrance gate, only opened after authorized personnel on that day's access orders were cleared for entrance into the facility. (Author's collection.)

Inside the security control center is a small arms weapons clearing barrel; it is the circle in the cabinet shown here. (Author's collection.)

If the freight elevator from the security control center is disabled, alternate access to the below-ground launch control equipment building and launch control center could be made by this steel ladder, which is enclosed inside a steel safety cage. (Author's collection.)

Primary access to the underground capsules was by freight elevator, for both personnel and equipment. The corridor shown here stops at a T-corridor to prevent direct access from a nuclear detonation. (Author's collection.)

Seen here is the blast door of the launch control equipment building, which provided backup environmental control and power to the launch control center if commercial power was disrupted. (Author's collection.)

The launch control center blast door is secured by 12 hydraulically operated latch pins around its perimeter. Entrance into the capsule requires one to duck through the low door, across a narrow walkway between the inner and outer steel capsule shell. (Author's collection.)

There are four of these large hydraulic shock absorbers that allow the capsule's suspended floor to move side-to-side without being destroyed, with all cables connected by flexible conduit. (Author's collection.)

Pictured is 1960s-era equipment, with the deputy missile combat crew commander's console in the center and the missile combat crew commander's console at the far end of the capsule. (Author's collection.)

This is a close-up view of the deputy missile combat crew commander's console. The box at upper-left contains the crew's missile launch keys, locked inside by two padlocks, with one for each missileer. (Author's collection.)

Shown is a close-up view of the missile combat crew commander's console, which monitored the 10 Minuteman missiles. (Author's collection.)

After 90 days in which the destroyed silo was left undisturbed for Russion intelligence verification, debris was bulldozed into the silo shaft, with surface bulldozed to level, returning it to grade as prior to construction. (Author's collection.)

The deactivated missile alert facility, declared excess federal property, was sold at public auction, with below-ground structures destroyed and filled in with no access, in compliance with the Strategic Arms Reduction Treaty. (Author's collection.)

Four

SAFEGUARD ANTI– BALLISTIC MISSILE SYSTEM
1967–1976

On November 3, 1967, the Department of Defense announced that Grand Forks AFB had been selected as a Sentinel anti–ballistic missile defense site, changed on March 14, 1969, to the Safeguard system, first constructed in the United States. The construction low bid was $137,858,850. The missile site radar site is located north of Nekoma, east on Highway 1 from Highway 5. It sits on 431 acres of land, divided into three sections: vacant land (201 acres), non-tactical area (118 acres) and tactical area (111 acres), with 30 long-range Spartan silos and 16 short-range, hypersonic Sprint silos. There were four remote Sprint launch sites (RSL-1 through 4). The final part of the Safeguard system is the perimeter acquisition radar (PAR) located in the northeast corner of the state; today, it is operational as the only remaining part of the anti–ballistic missile system at designated Cavalier Air Station, with a mission to track orbital targets. After the United States and the Soviet Union signed the Anti-Ballistic Missile Treaty of 1972, the United States retained its site at Grand Forks AFB when construction was completed on August 21, 1972, and it was turned over to the Army Safeguard Systems Command site activation team, followed by the PAR facility on January 3, 1973. The Safeguard Systems Command acquired the fourth and final remote launch site on November 5, 1972. It was named the Stanley R. Mickelsen Safeguard complex on June 21, 1974, and transferred to the US Army Safeguard Systems Command on September 3, 1974. On October 1, 1975, the Spartan and Sprint anti–ballistic missiles were fully operational. The next day, Congress ended operations of the anti–ballistic missile complex. The missile site radar went nonoperational in February 1976, with its equipment transferred to a secured storage depot. The Army removed the Spartan and Sprint missiles from their silos. The missiles were destroyed under compliance with the treaty, with a nonoperational missile retained as a museum or static display, and its nuclear warhead was removed and transported under guard to the Sierra Army Depot, California.

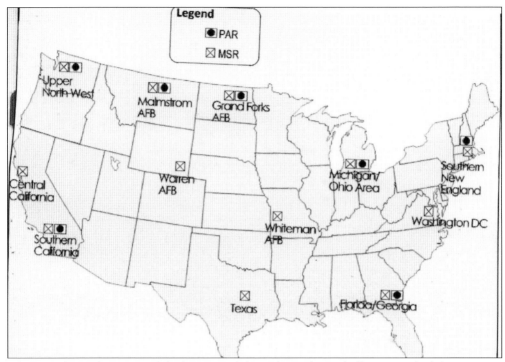

This map shows the proposed deployment of the Safeguard anti–ballistic missile defense system to create an airborne shield against incoming Russian ICBMs. Grand Forks AFB was the first and only operational Safeguard complex. (Courtesy of the US Army.)

Pictured is a two-stage, solid-fuel, hypersonic, point-defense Sprint anti–ballistic missile in the initial process of being lifted off its transporter/erector for positioning over a silo at Vandenberg AFB for a test launch. (Courtesy of the US Air Force.)

On display in the Langdon City Park of North Dakota is a two-stage, solid-fuel, supersonic, area-defense Spartan anti–ballistic missile. (Author's collection.)

The Safeguard anti–ballistic missile sites were positioned close to the US-Canadian border to intercept incoming Russian ICBMs as well as sufficiently separate so that one Russian warhead could not destroy them all, allowing survival due to hardened construction. (Courtesy of the National Register of Historic Places.)

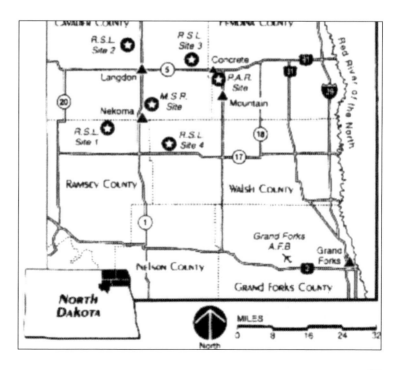

This aerial view of the Safeguard site at Nekoma, North Dakota, shows the missile site radar (top), Spartan anti–ballistic missile silos (center), and the Sprint anti–ballistic missile silos (bottom). (Courtesy of Grand Forks Air Force Base, 319th Air Base Wing Public Affairs.)

Pictured is a missile site radar tactical area—(1) commercial power substation, (2) auxiliary power plant, (3) heat sink, (4) control building, (5) underground entrance to site, (6) water reservoir, (7) Frequency Alignment Radar test antenna, (8) sentry station, (9) city of Nekoma, (10) access road, (11) universal missile assembly building, (12) missile sentry station, (13) security fencing, (14) warhead handling building, (15) Spartan silos, and (16) Sprint silos. (Courtesy National Register of Historic Places.)

The missile site radar building, nicknamed the "Pyramid," housed the huge phased-array radars and vacuum tube computers. (Author's collection.)

Pictured is the empty interior of the huge missile site radar building, with radars and computers removed, a shell deemed too expensive to demolish due to its construction to harden it to withstand a near-miss of a nuclear explosion. (Author's collection.)

The south entrance into the missile site radar building was protected with surrounding earth against a detonation and provided access for oversized equipment into the radar and auxiliary diesel-electric power room. (Author's collection.)

On top of the earth-covered concrete auxiliary diesel-electric power plant are these concrete structures. The tallest are exhausts for the power plant, and the shorter ones are air intakes for the diesel engines in the power plant. They were hardened to survive a nearby detonation. (Author's collection.)

This photograph shows the large area of the missile field for the site's 30 Spartan and 16 Sprint anti–ballistic missiles. There are onsite missile storage bunkers from which, if time permits, the silos can be reloaded and even shipped to the remote site launch complexes. (Author's collection.)

This close-up view of a Spartan anti–ballistic missile on display in the Langdon City Park shows the terminal guidance fins on the warhead/guidance package to direct the missile to the proper location to detonate its nuclear warhead. (Author's collection.)

Shown in this c. 2013 aerial photograph is the Cavalier Air Force Station, which is the site of the perimeter acquisition radar located in the northeast corner of North Dakota, west of the town of Concrete. (Courtesy of the US Geological Survey.)

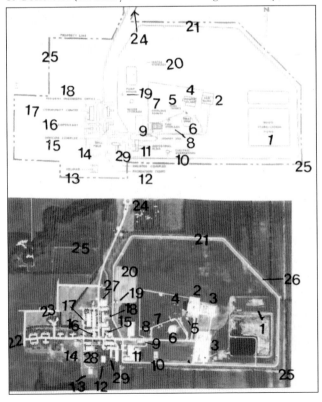

Pictured is the cavalier Air Force Station—(1) waste pond, (2) perimeter acquisition radar, (3) vehicle parking area, (4) power plant, (5) fuel tanks, (6) heat sink, (7) cooling tower, (8) fuel storage, (9) sentry station, (10) commercial electric sub-station, (11) industrial building, (12) recreation court, (13) helipad, (14) athletic field, (15) bachelor officers' housing, (16) dispensary, (17) community center, (18) engineering office, (19) pump house, (20) water storage, (21) security fencing, (22) three-bedroom duplexes, (23) three-bedroom housing units, (24) four-bedroom housing units, (25) security fencing, (26) patrol road, (27) fire station, (28) gym, and (29) enlisted barracks. (Courtesy of the US Air Force.)

Shown is the security access entry point into the PAR complex around 1973. The guard point personnel verified all security badges, allowing only authorized personnel into the site. (Courtesy of the US Air Force.)

Pictured is the northern face of the perimeter acquisition radar on Cavalier Air Force Station around 2013. (Author's collection.)

This photograph from 1973 shows enlisted barracks on the PAR site. This was replaced in December 2018 by a smaller, eight-person unaccompanied airmen dormitory. (Courtesy of the US Air Force.)

To support operation of the underground auxiliary diesel-electric power plant, hardened exhaust structures and shorter intact air structures were created. They were designed to withstand blast effects of a nearby nuclear detonation. (Author's collection.)

Pictured is the vehicle entrance to remote Sprint launch site No. 4, with the limited area sentry building to the far right and the underground earth-covered remote launch operations building to the left, with the tall concrete auxiliary diesel-electric exhaust on top of the building. (Author's collection.)

The limited area sentry building, with now-opened chain-link double portal access gates, controlled entrance into and exit from the remote Sprint launch site No. 4. (Author's collection.)

This is a view from the top of the earth-mounded, heavy grass-covered remote launch operations building down toward the limited area sentry control building and portal access dual security gates. (Author's collection.)

Shown is a side, north view of the remote launch operations building, with the concrete portal entrance down into the building. On top are the tall concrete exhaust and short air intake for the auxiliary diesel-electric generators. (Author's collection.)

This is a close-up view of the tall concrete exhaust tower for running the site's auxiliary diesel-electric generator. The auxiliary power plant was considered critical to maintaining uninterrupted operation during a nuclear exchange with the Soviet Union when commercial power could be destroyed, allowing launching of its 16 Sprint anti–ballistic missiles. (Author's collection.)

This is the bunkered entrance, with set-back twin steel blast doors, designed to protect the complex. The entrance faces east, so the north concrete side adds blast and debris protection from the effects of a near-miss by a nuclear detonation. (Author's collection.)

After passing through the bunkered entrance's steel blast doors, the passageway slopes downward. At its base in 2013, seeping water had accumulated to a depth of six to eight inches, because the sump pumps were no longer operational and there was no North Dakota environmental study to allow for the discharge of possibly polluted water. (Author's collection.)

Shown in 2013, this 1990s air-handling equipment brought in fresh air to the operations center while filtering out possible chemical, biological, and radioactive micro-particles into the building. Now, these are scrap and no longer operational. There is rust on all metal surfaces inside the building due to high humidity levels. (Author's collection.)

This view from the top of the remote launch operations building shows metal poles with high-intensity securing lighting, security perimeter fencing, and the adjacent sewage lagoon, not drained at this time, but with no influent allowed by the State of North Dakota. (Author's collection.)

Remote site launch site No. 4 is enclosed with double security fencing, with an additional double-security interior fencing surrounding the Sprint anti–ballistic missile underground silos. The entire area is covered by primary and secondary high-intensity security lighting to prevent unauthorized entrance. (Author's collection.)

At the rear of the launch site complex is a double-entry security gate and access control building into the 16 Sprint anti–ballistic missile silos and the missiles below, protected by fiberglass environmental covers. All missiles and equipment have been removed. (Author's collection.)

Here is a view of the four rows of four fiberglass-covered Sprint anti–ballistic missiles, inside double-security fencing with internal intrusion alarms and high-intensity lighting. Once all 16 Sprint missiles were fired, there was no on-site reload capability. If time permitted and the missile site radar complex survived, it might have been possible to deliver and reload the silos in preparation to defend against a second volley of Russian missiles. (Author's collection.)

This is a close-up photograph of four ground-mounted Sprint fiberglass silo coverings to protect them from nearby Russian nuclear detonation, thrusting out blast effects and debris over the site. (Author's collection.)

A Sprint anti–ballistic missile is slowly being lowered into a silo at Vandenburg AFB, California, for a test launch of the system from a specially designed and produced missile transporter and erector loader. (Author's collection.)

This view down into a Sprint anti–ballistic missile operational silo shows the rattle space between the silo's wall to protect it from severe shock waves from a nearby detonation, with flexible cables to provide communications, power, and monitoring from and to the remote launch site's command center. (Courtesy of the US Air Force.)

The United States has constructed a new, limited anti–ballistic missile defense shield against a possible Chinese or North Korean ICBM attack, which could threaten Alaska and the continental United States. Shown is the ground-based interceptor complex at Fort Greely, Alaska. (Courtesy of the US Army.)

This is an overhead view of the Fort Greely ground-based interceptor silos under construction. (Courtesy of the US Army.)

This transporter/erector trailer with a ground-based interceptor is moving toward a silo, where the missile will be positioned over the opening for loading. (Courtesy of the US Army.)

A ground-based interceptor positioned over an open silo is attached to two loading poles to allow the anti–ballistic missile to be slowly lowered into the silo without hitting the silo walls and damaging the missile. (Courtesy of the US Army.)

A ground-based interceptor is positioned at its silo at Vandenberg AFB, California. (Courtesy of the US Air Force.)

Five

WEAPONS STORAGE AREA
1956–2013

The Grand Forks AFB weapons storage area was located near the south perimeter of the base and east of the former SAC bomber and Boeing KC-135 Stratotanker alert area. It secured the Hound Dog air-ground missile carried by the Boeing B-52G Stratofortresses standing nuclear alert on the base, as well as free-fall gravity nuclear bombs, upgraded to short-range attack missiles and corresponding warheads. Convair F-106 Delta Darts carried the Genie air to air missiles, armed with a nuclear warhead. The weapons storage area stored warheads for the Minuteman II and III ICBMs, and for a short time, nuclear weapons carried by the North American B-1B Lancer. Warheads were also briefly stored for the Spartan and Sprint anti–ballistic missiles prior to installation in their silos or during swap-out of warheads. It was a busy facility with armed security forces convoys transporting Minuteman missiles and their warheads, especially during the removal of the 321st Missile Wing's missiles and warheads after deactivation. After the Strategic Arms Reduction Treaty, the weapons storage area reduced nuclear weapons storage until such weapons were eliminated. This was followed by the elimination of bombers on the base and the requirement to store conventional weapons for the B-1B, the last operational bomber variant on the base. The last B-1B departed the base in 1994 and the final Minuteman III warheads followed in 1998. When the B-1Bs were removed, comprehensive demolition of the 35 buildings inside the weapons storage area was conducted in three phases. Contract work consisted of demolition of buildings and foundations, with debris, utility lines, and remains of the buildings removed from the site. Once the area was graded, security fencing remained in place, with no guards, available for open area secure storage of non–weapons related equipment and materials such as construction materials for use on upgrading base infrastructure or modernization.

Pictured is the double security gate for the former weapons storage area, leading into the limited exclusion area, showing the security forces sentry station between the outer and inner chain link security gates. The gates are open in this photograph to allow heavy equipment and trucks removing the remains of the demolished structures to pass through. (Author's collection.)

Prior to entering the "Sally Port," the view to the left shows the site's power distribution poles and helicopter anti-intrusion poles to block unauthorized landings into the limited exclusion area. (Author's collection.)

Seen here are the remains of an earth-covered weapons storage igloo bunker after it was demolished, with concrete and steel ready to be hauled away for reuse and sale. (Author's collection.)

This photograph shows a modern, precision-guided munitions storage bunker used to store weapons to arm the bombers assigned to Grand Forks AFB with standoff air to ground missiles for nuclear deterrence alert missions. (Author's collection.)

Pictured is the security forces guard tower in the center of the former weapons storage area, which provided an unobstructed view throughout the limited security area. The observation booth is surrounded by a steel catwalk for observation or small arms use, if required. (Author's collection.)

Seen here is a close-up view of the security forces tower, equipped with communications equipment and a glass booth to protect personnel during inclement weather, allowing 24-hour protection of the nuclear weapons stored inside the site. (Author's collection.)

This tracked heavy backhoe was used by contractors to rip steel rebar away from torn-up concrete chunks from the demolished buildings. Excavation work was required before this work could begin and was completed prior to hauling away the debris. (Author's collection.)

Pictured is a large concrete building intact around 2013, at which time base officials had not determined any specific function for the building. (Author' collection.)

This is a view of a demolished earth-covered weapons storage igloo bunker, with an adjacent concrete building being demolished. (Author's collection.)

Demolition contractors used the following procedures: removal of earth covering material, hydraulic jackhammering by heavy equipment to break up the concrete structures, cutting torches to allow heavy backhoes to separate the concrete from the steel rebar, and hauling away the concrete rubble for reuse and the steel for scrap sale. (Author's collection.)

This is a view of part of the limited security area, with remaining power distribution poles and piles of demolished concrete structures prior to removal. (Author's collection.)

Seen here is the wide-angle view of part of the limited security area after demolition work had been completed. (Author's collection.)

This standard steel utility building inside the limited security area was retained for other functions as required to support base operations. (Author's collection.)

These two piles of concrete rubble are all that remain of the earth-covered, concrete igloo munitions storage bunkers. (Author's collection.)

Six

GLOBAL HAWK AND PREDATOR B

2011–PRESENT

The 69th Reconnaissance Group was activated on September 19, 2011, to perform aerial reconnaissance with unmanned aerial vehicles. It is equipped with the Northrop Grumman RQ-4 Global Hawk, a high-altitude, long-range, unmanned aircraft system with an integrated sensor suite that provides intelligence, surveillance, and reconnaissance capability world-wide. The Global Hawk's primary mission is to provide a broad spectrum of intelligence, surveillance, and reconnaissance collection capability to support joint combatant forces in worldwide peacetime, contingency, and wartime operations. The Global Hawk complements the US manned and space reconnaissance systems by providing persistent near–real time coverage using imagery intelligence and signal intelligence sensors. The Block 40 variants at Grand Forks carry the Radar Technology Insertion Program active electronically scanned array radar, which provides side aperture radar and ground moving target indicator data. The first Global Hawk was landed at Grand Forks AFB on May 26, 2011. On August 7, 2012, the 69th Reconnaissance Group flew its first Block 40 Global Hawk from the Grand Forks AFB runway. Up to this time, the unit only conducted flights remotely in an operational environment (overseas in undisclosed locations). The focus is on integrating the RQ-4 into the Grand Forks AFB flying rotation. Pilots of the 69th Reconnaissance Group fly daily operational missions over Afghanistan, remotely controlled from Grand Forks via satellite. US Customs and Border Protection operates the General Atomics MQ-9 Predator B at Grand Forks, beginning operations on December 6, 2008, when the first unmanned airframe arrived. The Predator B has been flown by CBP since 2005 over the southern US border with Mexico. Operating out of Grand Forks, CBP unmanned aerial vehicles enhance US-Canadian border security efforts and support its personnel operation on the ground along the border. The first operational mission for Grand Forks CBP's unmanned aerial vehicles was on August 12, 2008.

The first Northrop Grumman RQ-4 Global Hawk high-altitude, unmanned aerial reconnaissance vehicle to land at Grand Forks AFB, on May 26, 2011, is shown here, under tow for storage inside its hangar. (Courtesy of Grand Forks Air Force Base, 319th Air Base Wing Public Affairs.)

Pictured is a Global Hawk mission control element trainer. The pilot is on the left, and the sensor operator on the right. Both sit in comfortable chairs, with digital screens to remotely control and monitor the aircraft in a forward operating location. (Courtesy of the US Air Force.)

This view of a Global Hawk shows the engine air intake high-mounted at the rear of the whale-shaped fuselage, V-tail, thin wings, and retractable tricycle landing gear. (Courtesy of Grand Forks Air Force Base, 319th Air Base Wing Public Affairs.)

The Global Hawk is slowly being backed into a former Boeing KC-135 Stratotanker hangar. A ground crewman is positioned along the right side of the aircraft to place wheel chocks on one set of rear wheels once the aircraft is positioned inside the hangar. (Courtesy of Grand Forks Air Force Base, 319th Air Base Wing Public Affairs.)

Pictured is the Global Hawk launch recovery element, which supports the pilot and sensor operator during their operations shift. (Courtesy of the US Air Force.)

A Global Hawk is being backed tail first into its hangar prior to the aircraft being sent overseas for combat operations. (Author's collection.)

The Global Hawk's sensors, especially using infrared imaging, can maintain aerial reconnaissance 24 hours a day, in all weather conditions. Shown is a high-altitude infrared photograph of Naval Air Weapons Station China Lake, California. (Courtesy of Grand Forks Air Force Base, 319th Air Base Wing Public Affairs.)

This large-scale model of a Global Hawk unmanned aerial vehicle hangs from the ceiling in the main hallway of Grand Forks AFB Heritage Hall. (Author's collection.)

Shown is a General Atomics MQ-1B Predator, assigned to the CBP station at Grand Forks AFB to conduct aerial surveillance of the US-Canadian border. (Courtesy of Grand Forks Air Force Base, 319th Air Base Wing Public Affairs.)

This is an MQ-1B trainer, with the pilot on the left and sensor operator on the right. The image on the screen was taken in Iraq in 2005 and shows a pickup truck traveling on a road. The MQ-1B carries no weapons and is only equipped with sensors to monitor the US-Canadian border. (Courtesy of Grand Forks Air Force Base, 319th Air Base Wing Public Affairs.)

Launch and recovery or mission control responsibility

- Control the UAV through air traffic control (ATC) airspace
  - Usually 2-way UHF/VHF (voice)
- Primary responsibility is separation from other traffic - particularly manned aircraft (military and civil)
  - UAV control by line of sight, relay and/or SatCom data link

Global Hawk Mission Control Element

If required, the MQ-1B can be operated out of a deployable command center and trucked or flown to a forward operating airfield for border surveillance operations. (Courtesy of the US Air Force.)

At top is a head-on view of CBP MQ-9, showing its nose-mounted reconnaissance systems. On the bottom is an MQ-9 internal systems configuration. (Courtesy US Customs and Border Protection Public Affairs.)

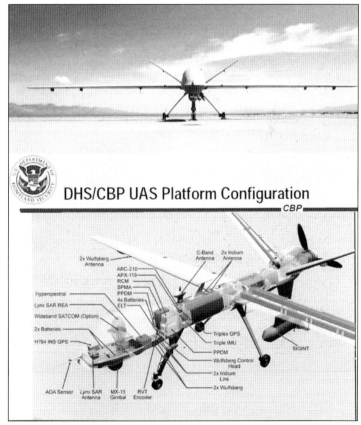

Construction began on the Grand Sky Business and Technology Park, a joint venture with Grand Forks AFB, by removing a section of the Cold War alert area concrete wall to provide direct access into the park from the adjacent highway to the south. (Courtesy of Grand Sky Development Company Public Affairs.)

This is the Grand Sky Technology Park's security entrance, where credentials for authorized workers and visitors are reviewed by a private security force. (Courtesy of Grand Sky Development Company Public Affairs.)

This is an overall view of the current Grand Sky Technology Park, with the Grand Forks AFB runway visible at upper right, which the park has access to via the former Cold War alert taxiway after clearance from the base control tower. (Courtesy of Grand Sky Development Company Public Affairs.)

Pictured is the completed Northrop Grumman facility in the Grand Sky Technology Park. (Courtesy of Grand Sky Development Company Public Affairs.)

This temporary hangar is used by Northrop Grumman for its commercial Global Hawk reconnaissance aircraft training facility until a permanent hangar is built. It serves as the nucleus for unmanned aerial vehicle research and development, with pilot, sensor operator, and maintainer training, along with operations and mission analysis and aircraft maintenance. (Courtesy of Grand Sky Development Company Public Affairs.)

Grand Sky Development Company has an agreement with North Dakota State University to serve as a mutual unmanned aerial vehicle training complex, as facilities are completed, such as in this conceptual planning drawing. (Courtesy of Grand Sky Development Company Public Affairs.)

This is a US Air Force armed Predator on the Ellsworth AFB flight line during an open house. Its profile, except for its munitions, is the same as that of CBP's MQ-9 at Grand Forks. (Author's collection.)

Here is a tail view of the armed Predator on the Ellsworth flight line during an open house, showing the pusher engine, V tail, thin wings, and fixed tricycle landing gear. (Author's collection.)

During a test by CBP, two MQ-9s taxi to takeoff positions for the first-ever dual training flight from Grand Forks AFB. (Courtesy of Grand Forks Air Force Base, 319th Air Base Wing Public Affairs.)

Grand Forks runway resurfacing is underway to repair wear from heavy B-52s and KC-135s during the Cold War, to allow safe unmanned aerial vehicle flight operations. (Courtesy of Grand Forks Air Force Base, 319th Air Base Wing Public Affairs.)

Seven

GRAND FORKS
AIR FORCE BASE AIR PARK
1983–PRESENT

Grand Forks AFB commanders decided to create an air park adjacent to the entrance to the base but outside the security fence to allow visitors access to historical aircraft on display. Even though the base was built after World War II as a Cold War air defense against Russian bombers, a SAC nuclear alert base, and the nation's only operational Safeguard anti–ballistic missile site, the roots of the current 319th Air Base Wing began in World War II. World War II aircraft on display honor the 319th Bombardment Group, which fought in that war. Air defense was an important part of the base's history, where Air Defense Command pilots stood 24-hour launch alert to intercept possible hostile aircraft. The air park displays Cold War aircraft that assisted the United States in maintaining nuclear deterrence and helped bring down the Berlin Wall and the former Soviet Union, helping to avert nuclear war during the Cuban Missile Crisis. Concrete walking paths allow visitors to walk among these historic aircraft and learn the history of Grand Forks AFB. Not everything is displayed, but there is enough to show the scope of those who made sacrifices from World War II to the present. Guided tours explaining the significance of each aircraft are available with two-week notice to 319th Air Base Wing Public Affairs.

The entrance to Grand Forks AFB consists of an inbound and outbound road with a central strip on the wide avenue containing all 50 state flags along with an adjacent air park on the north and south side. This is part of the base's extensive efforts to preserve its aviation history from World War II to the present. (Author's collection.)

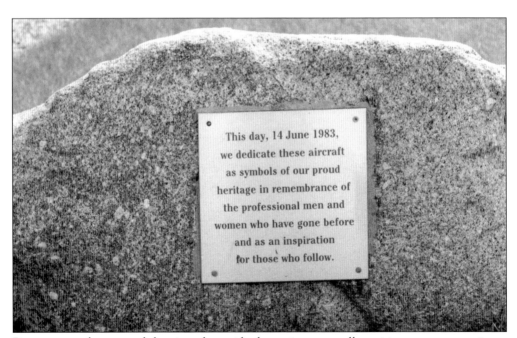

This day, 14 June 1983, we dedicate these aircraft as symbols of our proud heritage in remembrance of the professional men and women who have gone before and as an inspiration for those who follow.

Base commanders created the air park outside the main gate to allow visitors an opportunity to walk among some of the historic aircraft that helped maintain the nation's freedom from external threats. It was dedicated on June 14, 1983. (Author's collection.)

This model of a North American B-1B Lancer is mounted on top of a forward-swept pedestal to commemorate the assignment of this type of aircraft on Grand Forks AFB, from 1987 to 1993. (Author's collection.)

The Air Force used the Sikorsky HRS-1 (S-55) for search and rescue operations. The 321st Strategic Missile Wing used the helicopter to secure its 150 Minuteman launch facilites and 15 missile alert facilities, and to transport security forces to protect nuclear weapons movements and associated facilities. (Author's collection.)

The Bell UH-1N Iroquois "Huey" helicopter replaced the Sikorsky HRS-1 to support 321st Strategic Missile Wing's operations until July 2, 1988. (Author's collection.)

The 319th Air Base Wing's World War II history traces to the 319th Bombardment Group. The bomb group flew the Martin twin-engine Invader, produced at the Omaha, Nebraska, bomber plant. (Author's collection.)

On Grand Forks AFB, the 478th Fighter Wing, 18th Fighter-Interceptor Squadron flew the McDonnelll supersonic F-101 Voodoo in an air defense role from May 1960 to April 1971. (Author's collection.)

The air park contains a Minuteman III ICBM, which stood alert in the 150 launch facility silos around the base to perform instantaneous launch in response to a nuclear attack on the United States. (Author's collection.)

Pictured is a portable hydraulic lift aircraft control tower to be used if the main tower was disabled or nuclear alert operations moved to a dispersal airfield under high alert to a worsening period of relations that might result in a nuclear exchange. (Author's collection.)

Pictured is a North American twin-engine B-25 Mitchell bomber flown by the 319th Bombardment Group during World War II, from 1944 to the end of the war. (Author's collection.)

A Minuteman ICBM transporter/erector is attached to its prime mover, used to move missiles from Grand Forks AFB to and from the 321st Strategic Missile Wing's widely separated 150 launch facilities. (Author's collection.)

This Boeing B-52G Stratofortress heavy strategic bomber was assigned to Grand Forks from 1983 to 1986. (Author's collection.)

Pictured is a Hound Dog air-to-ground turbojet missile, two of which were carried by B-52Gs on nuclear alert on Grand Forks AFB. This is on display inside the base and not in the air park. (Author's collection.)

This Boeing KC-135A Stratotanker, the "City of Grand Forks," was the first tanker to land and be assigned to Grand Forks. (Author's collection.)

Eight

GRAND FORKS
AIR FORCE BASE

1956–PRESENT

Grand Forks AFB is a rare example of an Air Force base that was never an Army base, was built after World War II, and was named for a local community. Ongoing Cold War tensions led the Air Force to desire a northern and central observation and fighter-interception base. Grand Forks is located in the heart of the Red River Valley at the junction of the Red Lake River and the Red River of the North. The community has been ranked by *Money* magazine as one of the top in the nation. Grand Forks AFB plays a central role in the nation's defense. It is home to the 319th Air Base Wing, the only base in Air Mobility Command to receive remotely piloted aircraft systems, such as the RQ-4 Global Hawk unmanned aerial vehicle. The 319th Civil Engineers build, sustain, and protect real property, infrastructure, people, and the environment at Grand Forks AFB. The squadron sustains and repairs a $1.2 billion infrastructure that is comprised of 1,600 base personnel, 547 housing units, 220 facilities, and 344 dorm rooms, and executes a $15 million operating budget and $30 million construction program. The squadron oversees mission readiness and resources for environmental compliance, crash, fire, and rescue; weapons of mass destruction and disaster response; and recovery forces for the modernized base facilities. Grand Forks AFB, in 2018, generated approximately $286 million in local economic impact. Much of that went to local contractors for base construction projects on the Air Force's dollar, including $25 million on the taxiway, $3 million for gate upgrades, more than $600,000 toward the child development center, and $6.4 million on a Gray Hall dormitory renovation. The base does not resemble its Cold War beginnings; it is now a modern military installation comparable to surrounding North Dakota cities.

Warrior Inn on the base offers quality lodging to military personnel and their guests, including visitors' quarters, distinguished visitors' quarters, and temporary living facilities, with an in-house fitness center and Wi-Fi. (Author's collection.)

On base, there is unaccompanied housing for airmen E-1 to E-3 and E-4 with less than three years of active service. Each is provided a private sleeping room, furnishings, bed linens, and living supplies. (Author's collection.)

Accompanied base housing is run by a private management company, responsible for managing 600 family housing units, including 26 handicapped equipped units, with availability, location, and number of bedrooms determined by family size and rank. (Author's collection.)

1n 2014, as new housing units were completed, 31 older Cold War–era housing units were transported to Turtle Mountain Indian Reservation to meet housing needs there. (Courtesy of Grand Forks Air Force Base, 319th Air Base Wing Public Affairs.)

The Army Air Force Exchange Service Express features fuel pumps and a variety of shopping services. (Author's collection.)

The optometry, dental, and immunization clinic provides patient health care for base and retired personnel up to age 65. Transportation is provided by base ambulance to a civilian hospital emergency room. (Author's collection.)

The Community Activity Center offers a toddler room, giant play structure, small meeting room, large auditorium, and game/computer room. (Author's collection.)

The Commissary is a full-service grocery store carrying name brand goods. An adjacent Army Air Force Exchange Service is a retail sales outlet, with an Air Force military clothing sales outlet, alterations, dry-cleaning, barbershop and beauty services, and a food court. (Author's collection.)

Pictured is the Prairie Rose Chapel, provided for the worship needs of base airmen and their families in order to promote a healthy and spiritually resilient force. (Author's collection.)

The Airey dining facility is a world-class food service that can seat 228 personnel at once. It is open to all military and retired personnel, serving a wide variety of entrees, vegetables, salad bar, potato bar, pastries, and desserts. (Author' collection.)

The base fire station provides emergency response to aircraft accidents on the runway as well as fire protection for the base. (Author's collection.)

The fitness center maintains the physical fitness of the military population through exercise classes, weight room, organized sports, and weight control. (Author's collection.)

The base library has a large reference library, along with interlibrary loan capabilities, a reading room, a computer room, and a young children's reading room. (Author's collection.)

During renovation work on one of the former squadron operations buildings, a long-forgotten mural depicting Grand Fork's Boeing B-52G Stratofortress operations was discovered. It has been cleaned and is now displayed as part of the base's history. (Courtesy of Grand Forks Air Force Base, 319th Air Base Wing Historian.)

BIBLIOGRAPHY

"B-52Gs Assigned to Grand Forks Air Force Base." Omaha, Nebraska: Offutt Air Force Base, Strategic Command Historian Office.

"Chronology of Major Events—319th Air Base Wing (1942–2011)." Grand Forks Air Force Base, 319th Air Base Wing History Office, June 30, 2011.

"Grand Forks Air Force Base Safeguard Anti–Ballistic Missile Site construction." Grand Forks Air Force Base, 319th Air Base Wing Historian Office.

gsaauctions.gov

history.nd.gov. State Historical Society of North Dakota.

"Predator UAS Arrives at Grand Forks Air Force Base." Grand Forks Air Force Base, US Customs and Border Protection Public Affairs to 319th Air Base Wing Public Affairs.

www.strategic-air-command.com/missiles/Minuteman/Minuteman_Missile_Home_Page.htm.

Discover Thousands of Local History Books
Featuring Millions of Vintage Images

Arcadia Publishing, the leading local history publisher in the United States, is committed to making history accessible and meaningful through publishing books that celebrate and preserve the heritage of America's people and places.

Find more books like this at
www.arcadiapublishing.com

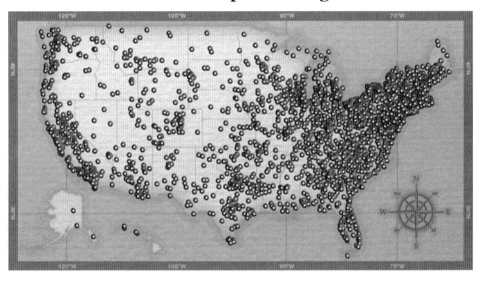

Search for your hometown history, your old stomping grounds, and even your favorite sports team.

Consistent with our mission to preserve history on a local level, this book was printed in South Carolina on American-made paper and manufactured entirely in the United States. Products carrying the accredited Forest Stewardship Council (FSC) label are printed on 100 percent FSC-certified paper.

MADE IN THE

USA